Gone Forever!
Brachiosaurus

Rupert Matthews

Heinemann
LIBRARY

www.heinemann.co.uk/library
Visit our website to find out more information about Heinemann Library books.

To order:

 Phone ++44 (0)1865 888066
 Send a fax to ++44 (0)1865 314091
Visit the Heinemann Bookshop at www.heinemann.co.uk/library to browse our catalogue
and order online.

First published in Great Britain by Heinemann Library, Halley Court, Jordan Hill, Oxford OX2 8EJ, a part of Harcourt Education. Heinemann is a registered trademark of Harcourt Education Ltd.

Editorial: Andrew Farrow and Dan Nunn
Design: Ron Kamen and Paul Davies and Associates
Illustrations: James Field of Simon Girling and Associates
Picture Research: Rebecca Sodergren and Ginny Stroud-Lewis
Production: Viv Hichens
Originated by Ambassador Litho Ltd
Printed and bound in China by South China Printing Company

07 06 05 04 03
10 9 8 7 6 5 4 3 2 1
ISBN 0 431 16617 X

British Library Cataloguing in Publication Data
Matthews, Rupert
Brachiosaurus. - (Gone forever)
1. Brachiosaurus - Juvenile literature
I. Title
567.9'12

Acknowledgements

The Publishers are grateful to the following for permission to reproduce copyright material: AKG pp. 12, 16, 18, 26; FLPA p. 14 (Mark Newman); Museum für Naturkunde, Berlin p. 20; Natural History Museum, London pp. 4, 6, 8, 10, 22, 24.

Cover photo reproduced with permission of Museum für Naturkunde, Berlin.

Our thanks to Dr Angela Milner of the Natural History Museum, London for her assistance in the preparation of this book.

Every effort has been made to contact copyright holders of any material reproduced in this book. Any omissions will be rectified in subsequent printings if notice is given to the Publishers.

Contents

Gone forever!. .4

The home of Brachiosaurus 6

The green valley. 8

In the shadow of Brachiosaurus. 10

What was Brachiosaurus? 12

Growing up. 14

The 'arm reptile'. 16

Reaching for food 18

Sharp teeth 20

Eating stones. 22

Under attack! 24

Fighting back. 26

Around the world 28

When did Brachiosaurus live?. 29

Fact file 30

How to say it 30

Glossary 31

Find out more. 32

Index 32

Some words are shown in bold, **like this**.
You can find out what they mean by looking in the Glossary.

Gone forever!

Sometimes all the animals of a particular type die. When this happens, the animal is said to have become **extinct**. Scientists study extinct animals by digging for **fossils**.

Allosaurus

Brachiosaurus

Kentrosaurus

One extinct animal was Brachiosaurus. This was a **dinosaur** that lived about 150 million years ago. Other types of creatures lived at the same time as Brachiosaurus. Nearly all the animals that lived then have become extinct.

The home of Brachiosaurus

Brachiosaurus **fossils** have been found in rocks. Scientists called **geologists** study these rocks. The rocks can show what the area was like when Brachiosaurus lived there.

Some Brachiosaurus fossils were found in Africa in 1927.

Brachiosaurus lived in places where the land was flat. There was plenty of water. The weather was warm all year round. Some seasons were wet and some seasons were dry.

The green valley

Scientists have found **fossil** plants in the same rocks as Brachiosaurus fossils. The fossil plants show them what plants grew when Brachiosaurus was living. Some of these plants were similar to those that grow today. Others were very different.

fossil of a plant

Brachiosaurus lived in open country. There were
many trees growing in small groups. Some were
pine and fir trees that looked quite like modern
trees but were much smaller. Some of the plants
that grew then are now **extinct**.

In the shadow of Brachiosaurus

Compsognathus fossil

The **fossils** of beetles and other insects have also been found in the rocks. This shows they lived at the same time as Brachiosaurus. There are also fossils of small **mammals** that looked like **shrews**.

A tiny **dinosaur** called **Compsognathus** lived in the thick undergrowth. It hunted mammals, **lizards** and **insects**. Compsognathus was about 1 metre long. It weighed about the same as a large chicken.

What was Brachiosaurus?

Scientists study the **fossil skeletons** of Brachiosaurus. The fossils show that Brachiosaurus was a huge creature. It was about 23 metres long and may have weighed up to 80 tonnes!

Brachiosaurus was one of the largest animals ever to live on the Earth. Scientists believe it probably walked very slowly. They know that it ate plants, such as leaves from trees.

Growing up

Fossils of young **dinosaurs** similar to Brachiosaurus have been found. Scientists believe that Brachiosaurus was probably only one metre long when it first hatched. Perhaps Brachiosaurus hatched from eggs like these.

dinosaur egg fossils

It is possible that young Brachiosaurus hid from meat-eating dinosaurs in thick undergrowth. The undergrowth would also have provided plenty of food for the young. Young Brachiosaurus may also have travelled with adults as part of a **herd**.

The 'arm reptile'

The name Brachiosaurus means 'arm-reptile'. The **dinosaur** was given this name because its front legs are longer than its back legs. Most dinosaurs had longer back legs than front legs.

The long front legs of Brachiosaurus carried the weight of the long neck and head. Powerful shoulder **muscles** kept the dinosaur's head upright. Other muscles moved the legs.

17

Reaching for food

The neck bones of Brachiosaurus were strong, but light. They had large holes in them. This made them less heavy. The bumps on the neck bones were attached to strong **muscles**. The muscles moved the head and neck.

fossil of Brachiosaurus neck bones

Fossil bones show that Brachiosaurus held its neck upright. This meant it could reach leaves and twigs at the tops of trees. Most dinosaurs could not reach this food. Brachiosaurus and a few other dinosaurs had it all to themselves.

Sharp teeth

Brachiosaurus teeth were large and strong. These teeth were good for stripping tough leaves from plants. Scientists have found the teeth are badly worn. This means Brachiosaurus bit through very tough plants.

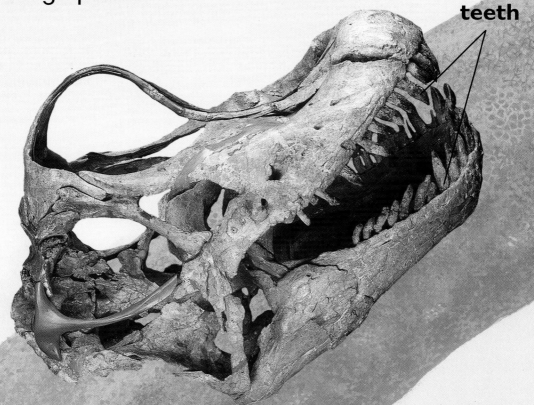

teeth

Brachiosaurus skull

Brachiosaurus probably ate by snapping its jaws
shut on plants and then pulling. It would have bitten
off chunks of leaves and twigs and swallowed them
whole. Brachiosaurus did not chew its food.

21

Eating stones

Scientists who dig up Brachiosaurus and similar **fossils** occasionally find piles of stones nearby. These stones have been worn smooth. They are called 'gastroliths', which means 'stomach stones'.

Brachiosaurus sometimes swallowed stones. These stones stayed in the **dinosaur's** stomach. They pounded against the leaves eaten by the dinosaur. This turned the plants into a mushy paste, which could be easily **digested**.

23

Under attack!

Scientists have found the **fossils** of a large meat-eating **dinosaur**. They have named this dinosaur Allosaurus. Allosaurus was a hunter that lived at the same time as Brachiosaurus. It had sharp claws and teeth. It attacked and killed other dinosaurs.

sharp teeth

Allosaurus skull

Allosaurus was up to twelve metres long. Scientists think it might have attacked young Brachiosaurus that were small and easy to kill. If several Allosaurus worked together they might have been able to kill an **adult** Brachiosaurus.

25

Fighting back

Brachiosaurus had a large, sharp claw on its front foot. Some scientists think it used this claw to protect itself from attack. It might also have been used to stop Brachiosaurus from slipping.

claw

Perhaps Brachiosaurus tried to injure attackers using its large claw. Or Brachiosaurus may have tried to crush attackers by stomping on them. Larger, older Brachiosaurus were less likely to be attacked.

27

Around the world

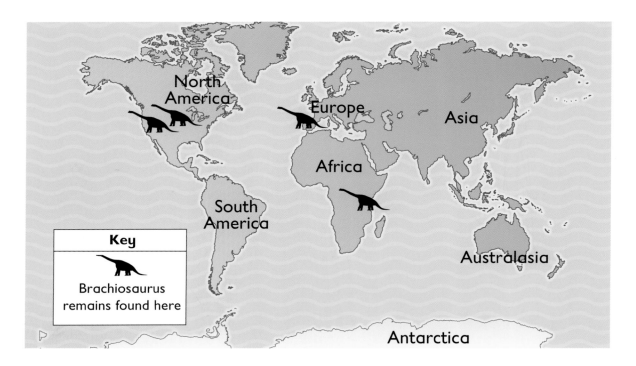

The **fossils** of Brachiosaurus have been found in North America, East Africa and Western Europe. At the time of Brachiosaurus these **continents** were joined together. There was no Atlantic **Ocean**. The dinosaurs could have moved from one continent to the other.

When did Brachiosaurus live?

Brachiosaurus existed for just a few million years, about 150–140 million years ago (mya). They lived in the middle of the Age of the Dinosaurs, which scientists call the Mesozoic Era. Many other large dinosaurs with long necks and tails lived at about the same time. These are known as **sauropods**.

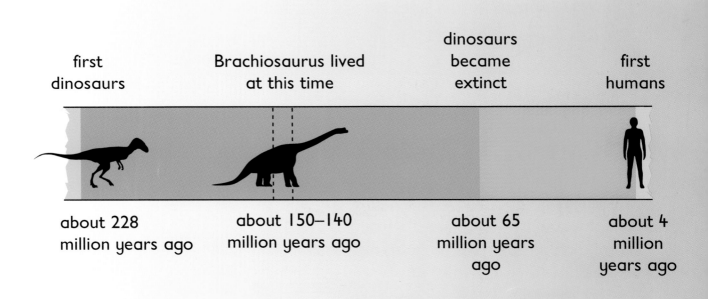

first dinosaurs	Brachiosaurus lived at this time	dinosaurs became extinct	first humans
about 228 million years ago	about 150–140 million years ago	about 65 million years ago	about 4 million years ago

Fact file

Brachiosaurus fact file	
Length:	about 23 metres
Height:	up to 14 metres
Weight:	up to 80 tonnes
Time:	Late Jurassic Period, about 150–140 million years ago
Place:	North America, Africa, Europe

How to say it

Allosaurus – al-oh-saw-rus
Brachiosaurus – brak-ee-oh-saw-rus
Compsognathus – komp-sogg-nay-thus
dinosaur – dine-oh-saw

Glossary

adult grown up

Compsognathus one of the smallest dinosaurs. It hunted mammals and other small animals.

continents large mass of land, such as Europe or Africa

digested food that has been broken into tiny pieces so it can be used by the body

dinosaurs reptiles that lived on Earth between 228 and 65 million years ago. Dinosaurs are extinct.

extinct an animal is extinct when there are none left alive

fossils remains of a plant or animal, usually found in rocks

geologist a scientist who studies rocks is called a geologist

herd group of animals living and travelling together

insect small creature with a hard outer covering and six legs

lizard small reptile with four legs

mammal animal with hair or fur. Mammals give birth to live young instead of laying eggs.

muscles parts of an animal's body that provide power to make it move

ocean very large area of sea

sauropods four-legged dinosaurs which ate plants and had long necks and tails

shrew type of small mammal with a long nose

skeleton bones that support the body of an animal

Find out more

These are some other books about dinosaurs:
Big Book of Dinosaurs, Angela Wilkes (Dorling Kindersley, 2001)
Brachiosaurus, Michael Goecke (Abdo Publishing, 2002)
Dinosaur Park, Nick Denchfield (Macmillan, 1998)

Look on these websites for more information:
www.bbc.co.uk/dinosaurs/fact_files/scrub/brachiosaurus.shtml
www.enchantedlearning.com/subjects/dinos/Brachiosaurus.shtml
www.oink.demon.co.uk/topics/dinosaur.htm

Index

claws 26–27
food 13, 15, 19, 20–21
fossils 4, 6, 8, 10, 12, 14, 19, 24
home 7, 9, 15, 28, 30
legs 16–17
neck and head 17, 18
other animals 10–11, 14,
   24–25, 27
plants 8–9, 13, 19, 20–21
rocks 6, 8

size 12–13, 30
stomach stones 22–23
teeth 20
weather 7
young Brachiosaurus 14–15, 25

Titles in the *Gone Forever* series include:

Hardback	0 431 16604 8
Hardback	0 431 16616 1
Hardback	0 431 16602 1
Hardback	0 431 16605 6
Hardback	0 431 16614 5
Hardback	0 431 16601 3
Hardback	0 431 16600 5
Hardback	0 431 16615 3
Hardback	0 431 16603 X

Find out about the other titles in this series on our website www.heinemann.co.uk/library